Wes Gets Wet

by Emma Green
illustrated by Len Epstein

Core Decodable 46

McGraw Hill Education

Bothell, WA • Chicago, IL • Columbus, OH • New York, NY

MHEonline.com

Send all inquiries to:
McGraw-Hill Education
8787 Orion Place
Columbus, OH 43240

ISBN: 978-0-02-130695-4
MHID: 0-02-130695-8

Printed in the United States of America.

9 10 11 12 KOD 24

Gwen scrubs Dad's truck.
Wes trots to help.

Gwen tells Wes to sit next to the wall.
Will Wes get wet there?

Gwen waxes the truck.
Wes sits and twitches.

Wes sits and sits.

The wind grabs a twig.
Wes jumps and runs. Wes is swift!

The twig went. Wes is wet, and Gwen is wet!